Right To

N_{on}

R_{eligious}

C_{iti}

I0791160

~~Hindu, Buddhist, Muslim, Christians, Sikh, Jain, Others~~

#IamNRC

By

W. Hoami

ii

ISBN: 978-1-6586-2453-4

What is your RELIGION?

HINDU / MUSLIM / CHRISTIAN / Others

CONTENTS

ACKNOWLEDGMENT

Sometimes thousands of lines mean nothing.

Sometimes one line means everything.

You found me,

You are special.

I offer my humble offering to you.

_ W. Hoami

CHAPTER 1

TWO QUESTIONS

Q. Do you want to select Religion

consciously?

Q. Do you want to remove the stamp

you got unwillingly at the time of

your birth?

CHAPTER 2

INTRODUCTION

Let religion be blissful

Let religious be conscious.

Your 'birth of consciousness' did not occur at your will.

Don't you think your 'will' should be free until and unless that disrupts the 'free-will' of another 'free-willed' person???

At birth, you cannot select:

1. Parents

2. Place of birth

3. Gender

4. Name

5. Religion

6. Caste / category etc.

But

After gaining consciousness you should be

able to select your own:

1. Name

2. Religion

3. Caste / category etc.

Right To Non-Religious Citizen (NRC)

CHAPTER 3:

Essence
of
Free World's
Constitution

1st draft

01.01.2020

*"Our planet is so rich.
Everyone should live like King & Queen"*

When planet Earth is obliterating some part of herself by some other part of herself the mode is always through the clash of belief, ego, possessiveness of material and humans, etc.

Whenever those acts were over the executioner of that thought may be given second chance.

Humans may always get chances to metamorphose from its past form.

They should be able to change their name, location, identity, bonds with other humans.

Possessiveness of all kinds if given up by us.

Then we shall all be truly free.

One country - WORLD

No ownership over anything or anyone

No name

No religion

No identity

No owned home

No dependencies

No scarcity

No rich

No poor

No son

No daughter

No father

No mother

No husband

No wife

No friends

No social policing

No taboos

No pain

No suffering

No hunger

No state boundaries

No records for human

Free sex on mutual consent

Free education

Free health care

Free old age care

Free infant care

Free shelter

Free transportation

Right to Knowledge

Right to Live

Right to Change of Identity (COI)

Right to Non-Religious Citizenship (NRC)

Right to No Caste (RNC)

Right to deletion of past records (RDPR)

Right to Painless Death (RPD)

True Free world.

In this book, we shall only discuss

Right **T**o

Non

Religious

Citizen

CHAPTER: 4

(Existing)

Right to

Freedom of Religion

as on 01.01.2020

[Article 25, 26, 27, 28 of Indian Constitution]

Article 25: Freedom of conscience and free profession, practice and propagation of religion.

(1) Subject to public order, morality, and health and to the other provisions of this Part, all persons are equally entitled to freedom of conscience and the right freely to profess, practice and propagate religion.

(2) Nothing in this article shall affect the operation of any existing law or prevent the State from making any law—

(a) regulating or restricting any economic,

financial, political or other secular activity which may be associated with religious practice;

(b) providing for social welfare and reform or the throwing open of Hindu religious institutions of a public character to all classes and sections of Hindus.

Explanation I.—The wearing and carrying of kirpans shall be deemed to be included in the profession of the Sikh religion. Explanation II.—In sub-clause (b) of clause (2), the reference to Hindus shall be construed as including a reference to persons professing the Sikh, Jaina or Buddhist religion, and the reference to Hindu religious institutions shall be construed accordingly.

Article 26: Freedom to manage religious affairs.

Subject to public order, morality and health, every religious denomination or any section thereof shall have the right—

(a) to establish and maintain institutions for religious and charitable purposes;

(b) to manage its own affairs in matters of religion;

(c) to own and acquire movable and immovable property; and

(d) to administer such property in accordance with the law.

Article 27: Freedom as to payment of taxes for promotion of any particular religion.

No person shall be compelled to pay any taxes, the proceeds of which are specifically appropriated in payment of expenses for the promotion or maintenance of any particular religion or religious denomination.

Article 28: Freedom as to attendance at religious instruction or religious worship in certain educational institutions.

(1) No religious instruction shall be provided in any educational institution wholly maintained out of State funds.

(2) Nothing in clause (1) shall apply to an educational institution which is administered by the State but has been established under any endowment or trust which requires that religious instruction shall be imparted in such institution.

(3) No person attending any educational institution recognized by the State or receiving aid out of State funds shall be required to take part in any religious instruction that may be imparted in such institution or to attend any religious worship that may be conducted in such

institution or in any premises attached thereto unless such person or, if such person is a minor, his guardian has given his consent thereto.

Right To Non-Religious Citizen (NRC)

Article 25: Freedom of conscience and free profession, practice and propagation of religion.

(1) Subject to public order, morality, and health and to the other provisions of this Part, all persons are equally entitled to freedom of conscience and the right freely to profess, practice and propagate religion.

(2) Nothing in this article shall affect the operation of any existing law or prevent the State from making any law—

(a) regulating or restricting any economic, financial, political or other secular activity which may be associated with religious

CHAPTER: 6

(PROPOSED)

Right to
Freedom
of
Religion

[Article 25, 26, 27, 28 of

Indian Constitution]

As per the census of India, almost 0.7 % of India's population belongs to the "Others" category under the "Religion" column of the census.

There may be many who want to opt for "NO RELIGION", however, they cannot do so because of the fact that there are no such options.

It seems like they got irreversible stamped at the time of birth.

Need not to say that human beings are identified, sorted, prioritized, divided on the basis of religion.

Chapter: 5

NEED FOR

THE

AMENDMENTS

practice;

(b) providing for social welfare and reform or the throwing open of Hindu religious institutions of a public character to all classes and sections of Hindus.

Explanation I — The wearing and carrying of kirpans shall be deemed to be included in the profession of the Sikh religion. Explanation II.—In sub-clause (b) of clause (2), the reference to Hindus shall be construed as including a reference to persons professing the Sikh, Jaina or Buddhist religion, and the reference to Hindu religious institutions shall be construed accordingly.

(3) If any person wants to be a NON-RELIGIOUS CITIZEN he/she shall be

allowed to be so.

(4) No one shall be needed to give out the information regarding their religious status to any State-aided or any other person or organization or employer or religious group for whatsoever the purpose may be, in any form.

(5) No identity proof or certificate or documents of any persons or place shall mention any religious status.

(6) Every person shall have the right to select their religion of conscious choice only after the attainment of 21 years of age.

Article 26: Freedom to manage religious affairs.

Subject to public order, morality and health, every religious denomination or any section thereof shall have the right—

(a) to establish and maintain institutions for religious and charitable purposes;

(b) to manage its own affairs in matters of religion;

(c) to own and acquire movable and immovable property; and

(d) to administer such property in accordance with the law.

Article 27: Freedom as to payment of taxes for promotion of any particular religion.

No person shall be compelled to pay any taxes, the proceeds of which are specifically appropriated in payment of expenses for the promotion or maintenance of any particular religion or religious denomination.

Article 28: Freedom as to attendance at religious instruction or religious worship in certain educational institutions.

(1) No religious instruction shall be provided in any educational institution wholly maintained out of State funds.

Right To Non-Religious Citizen (NRC)

CHAPTER: 7

How to be an NRC ?

By passing an amendment bill in the constitution about Article 25 to 28.

CHAPTER: 8

How to pass an Amendment Bill

What is social media?

Social media is a form of a communication platform that connects people through the internet; irrespective of caste, creed, economic & social status.

Used by almost everyone from common people to the leaders of nations.

CHAPTER 9:

A pledge

by

Worldians

The World is my country;

All Worldians are my brothers and sisters.

I love my World,

And

I am proud of its rich and varied heritage.

I shall always strive to be worthy of it.

I shall respect my parents, teachers and all

elders and treat everyone with courtesy.

To my World and my people,

I pledge my devotion.

In their well-being and prosperity lies my

happiness.

ABOUT THE AUTHOR

About me:

I am ignorant of my origin.
I don't remember I was born.

I was told that I was born.
I am told that I shall die.

I don't believe both.
When I ask myself.

I know.

Pain is true.
Death is a lie.
And I shall never die.

_ W. Hoami

About you:

You may believe you know your origin.

But you don't remember you were born.

You were told that you were born.

You were told that you shall die.

You may believe both.

Call my name.

You shall know.

Pain is true.

Death is a lie.

And you too shall never die.

_ W. Hoami

Right To Non-Religious Citizen (NRC)

What is your RELIGION?

HINDU / MUSLIM / CHRISTIAN / Others /

NRC